BY THE SAME AUTHOR

Poetry

The Oath and Amen

America Is a Punjabi Word

An Old Chair

My Second in Kentucky

This Time in Lahore

Neither This Time/Nor That Place

Inland and Other Poems

The Poems of Alamgir Hashmi

Sun and Moon and Other Poems

A Choice of Hashmi's Verse

The Ramazan Libation

Literary Criticism

Commonwealth Literature

Ezra Pound

The Commonwealth, Comparative Literature and the World

Edited Anthologies

Pakistani Literature: The Contemporary English Writers

The Worlds of Muslim Imagination

Pakistani Short Stories in English

Post-Independence Voices in South Asian Writings

Your Essence, Martyr

THE SHORTER POEMS
1993-2023

THE SHORTER POEMS
1993-2023

ALAMGIR HASHMI

GREENWICH EXCHANGE
LONDON

Greenwich Exchange, London

First published in Great Britain in 2024
All rights reserved

The Shorter Poems 1993-2023
© Aurangzeb Alamgir Hashmi, 2024

This book is sold subject to the conditions that it shall not, by way of trade or otherwise, be lent, resold, hired out or otherwise circulated without the publisher's prior consent in any form of binding or cover other than that in which it is published and without a similar condition including this condition being imposed on the subsequent purchaser.

Printed and bound by imprintdigital.com
Cover design by December Publications
Tel: 07951511275

Greenwich Exchange Website: www.greenex.co.uk

Cataloguing in Publication Data is available
from the British Library

ISBN: 978-1-910996-77-5

To the loving memory of my parents
who read or recited poetry nearly every day

Go, litel bok ...
– *Geoffrey Chaucer*

Go, lovely rose!
– *Edmund Waller*

CONTENTS

Tropics *17*

Diary *19*

According to the Scriptures *21*

Taxila / Margalla *22*

For Children in Wartime *24*

People *26*

L'Objet Trouvé *29*

Salaam to Ts'ai Lun *33*

Line Rent *34*

The City Not Being Us *36*

In Praise of Linseed *37*

Linseed: An Anniversary *38*

Ban *39*

N.B. *42*

Arrival *44*

Suggestion *45*

There *46*

In Iceland *47*

Summer is Here *48*

Laura *50*

Ne Plus Ultra *51*

'Any Ideas?' *52*

Birds in a Tree: An Elegy *55*

Off the Expressway *56*

Being There *57*

Sonnet After the Tsunami *59*

Above Balakot *60*

It Was Quaking-Grass Awhile *61*

New Orleans, 2005 *62*

Earthworms *63*

Sister Cities *64*

No End to Summer *65*

Between the Rivers *66*

To a Query *68*

The City without Footpaths *69*

'Stars to Grieve at Pavarotti Funeral' *70*

Beds in the East *71*

Woodpeckers *72*

Composition in Early Winter *73*

Now, Now *74*

Camp Office *75*

Composition in Early Summer *76*

First Information *77*

Northern Valleys *80*

'Slain Workers Undaunted' *81*

Rescue *82*

At Eighty-Six *84*

How Pale the First Moon of the Year *85*

Post *87*

Not Moving *88*

East River *89*

Josephus' Footnote to Historia *90*

Tryst *91*

Amusements for Elinor White *92*

Numbers *93*

Still Life *94*

Happenings *95*

Peonies *97*

God Said, Let There Be an End *98*

Enlisted *100*

Occasion *101*

River Poem *102*

Crossing the Alps *104*

All Too Often a Grey Boulder Rolls Down *105*

Spring at the Door *107*

City, West *109*

They Say, They Never Wrote *111*

Garbage News *112*

Facts *114*

Adam's Peak *116*

Everyday *118*

So Welcome, Fuzzy Winter Light *120*

Conversation *122*

Fest *124*

What Do You Know? *126*

Your Dad *127*

Sides *128*

Bulrushes, Normandy *129*

S Again *130*

Odesville *131*

Grouse *133*

Sweet Water Only *135*

Virus Regulation *137*

Budget Speech *145*

Epistle *147*

Missing Subjects *151*

A Reckoning *152*

Billy's World *154*

Testing Ground *155*

Onward *156*

Sheltering in Place *157*

Montana *159*

Index of Titles

Acknowledgements

Biography

TROPICS

Supple –
branches of the mulberry –
were her arms,
free and warm,
swaying in the summer wind.

I held down a branch to one side,
    gathered the fine mass of leaves
    in my hand, lifted up,
and tongued into the ripeness.

The crow in the tree shouted:
 this is not a mistletoe-toe-toe.

    Peaches!
And all was pulsing under the gold-
beaten bark;
custom had made her bold.
    She kissed me until the South Pole
    ice began to shift,
explorer ships blew their banjo horns
and the season turned.
The sky had more light.

Was it the date-palm overhead
dropping its divine fruit to the ground?
Or the peach,
adding to sweetness, plumped down?
Either, we ate to refocus time.

But the sky's looks
still fall on us hard as hailstones
as we dream our dream
of tasting winter the summer way –
impeachment of ice-cream.

DIARY

The hibiscus at noon wags a red tongue
from the courtyard wall;
its invitations are sidelined
for the topical quisqualis
in the gateway – a
fragrance that agrees with everyday,
mild, unimpeachable
till the dead of night,
when it is not itself
(or perhaps is).
The red blossom cupped in my hands later,
in the thirsty afternoons,
blows to springtide;
(leggings drop away like the hours).
Succulent, this nethertongue
is a flower in my mouth,
is a fountain,
is the words I utter.
You say, I'm spilling over.
In the evenings you put lemongrass
in the tea: the aroma will bring
me back to the same: touch off the unsaid.
The conversation
turns to how it was or could be.
Memory is a leaf
in the wind, arising.
Autumn nights, whatever splashes
against the streetlight is rainwater,
or the soundless penny dropped
in the wishing well.

You say, it's the blind spots of time.
In the dark, I think of this sound again.
Perhaps you will not wait;
you will light a candle
before the words inflame.

ACCORDING TO THE SCRIPTURES

Just weeks before the last frost
of spring, in equal rows I sow,
back and forth, in the rich loamy soil,
as both the Qur'an and Shakespeare
suggest I plough
this, my farm, well; and reap from its toil
a respite from the sun-drawn thirst,
until the leaves meet between the rows
and completely shade me in the ground.
Then a stem rises high enough,
bearing numerous yellow flowers.
It is time.
I bend over and kiss your turnips,
flattened, white-fleshed, loamy,
pink and then purple to touch, warm;
and they grow, upturn, invert
in the mouth – crowned
each by
a nipple.

TAXILA / MARGALLA

Licked off the ground with tongues of steel
or crushed into stone floors
of these neo-Islamic houses
and the uptight slate of roads driven,
they cry with tears as big as boulders
rolling down their dark cheeks.
The umbilicus is cut;
the earth's gashes are ever-new,
unhealed: it rises here and there
with its amphoras for holding lovers
like liquid, surplus grain; to envelop
and conceal a maze of fine-ticking cities
from the wanton gaze of time –
future's the worst that could happen.
Now these leftover mountains
are moving away from here
on nervous feet,
looking askance,
for safety is in moving on.
Where they will go, split what country,
joint which continents – America
with Asia to repatriate Columbus? –
no one is in the know. What-
ever be the case, their silence is proverbial,
glistening old as the language
removing shard and reject,
or the edges of obsidian
from its thought.
Each hiking trail winces
at my approaching steps;

birds sound warning cries;
shrubs green out and get in the way
flaring like autumn leaves.

FOR CHILDREN IN WARTIME

This is the art class.
The theme of the lesson
is Sarajevo in springtime.
On a sheet of A4 appears a street
with its men and women
                     scattered
on their backs;
red balloons
from their insides
        pop
on the pavement.
Cars in the background
are shot full of holes.
The artist is twelve and a half.

In her neighbour's piece,
a zigzag across the window
is perhaps a smashed windshield.
The roof is literally flying
off one house,
a twist of orange flame
spiralling upwards.

A hush descends as twenty
small heads bend over
a fresh set of drawings.
Doors, closed,
have the faces of people frightened.
Trees weep out tears the size of snowdrops.

A pair of spectacles lies on the street,
next to a man with closed eyes
looking very dead.
But that's not me, hearing still
the mortar level the walls,
sniper bullet hit
somewhere across the courtyard.
Cities are going
but what's to hold up a wax crayon?
Children know
that pictures cannot be stretched too far.
School's in progress
as if it were a prayer –
about how it was supposed to be.

Just six feet from me
the lawn's growing wild
below the daily reticent
                    jasmine;
each blade an argument
of this season's excesses.
Without raiders, this street is fine.
But, alas. I too can't
write from the point of view of grass.

PEOPLE
for the Sondhis

From Kashmir you came to Lahore
to wed this handsome man of economics
(come from Jullundur, via Indore)
who played Hamlet in the same breath
as he lectured to fix
each flower in its place
in the College gardens,
expecting they would nod ever
to the lightest breeze
with an English sense of purpose.
Even the winter terms were pleasant.
Hockey matches could warm the spirit
as in the Forties nearly each stick
trained for the penalty stroke.
Evenings were rose-walks and tea.
It was this knowledge –
life held together by choice, where one is
and will be, within a peashooting chance.

Come 1947 podding to fruit and fall away,
the vegetal crease split,
seed and flower scatter by the hour.
The College clock, no matter how
you rewind it, rarely agrees
with Pakistan Standard Time.
The fountain named after you vents bubbles
of some ghostly speech no play-actor can use.

Anyway, you two that side of the border,
christian-and-hindu visited sometimes here
your muslim daughters happy in their
families. Thus years went sliding
like the snow round your hill-house
between Simla and Kasauli.
You were away then briefly.
Those sweet-scented flowers you left for him
were snuffed out in his sunless room.
He was asleep,
buried where the harsinghar
sheds its flowers
timely.

You changed country again,
back in Lahore to what connects you –
no, not the land that deludes
its own voice, but one last inflection,
the stem stitch of family – serial views
of just how it should be:
your daughters to their husbands objured,
the grandchildren and great-grandchildren
growing, filling in like houseplants, pets.
What you lost of them you would not see.
Pain was the only potion you knew
which could overcome the memory.
Today, in your blue-cushioned chair
waiting for tea, about to comb your hair,
you take your final leave.
Your husband dead elsewhere,
the gods, still vigilant, claim you,
each in his own name:

you were courteous;
your grace now beyond question.
Parishioner, priest and passer-by all know
the right words to action, your body below.

As if you had wished it, on this bright
spring day, a thoughtful tahli
bow-waves a kindly shade;
imprinting here what you see, can't see.
A shower of rose-petals slowly
fades in the fresh earth.
Over and over they come, settle down.
This must be the way love is made.

Note: G.D. Sondhi, founder of Asian Games and first Indian Principal (1939-1945) of Government College, Lahore, died in Simla (India) in 1966. His widow, Enid Lila Sondhi, died in Lahore (Pakistan) in 1995.

L'OBJET TROUVÉ
for Babar, who found me it

There I lay in the wild.
The grasses grew around me
green while the rain fell
drop following shadow drop
and the autumn's returning
auburn far away.
I must have looked
like deadwood
among the file of stumps
and charred saplings spared by bushfires;
a useless broken limb
of a limb
broken off a limb of something
       like a proper tree,
a poplar with branches splayed out
       in supplication for more light,
       every leaf tremulous to the sou'wester;
an aspen still at the landsliding Kashmir.
Or perhaps a mere yarrow in the uplands
that had known a summer
or two and was knocked down by one.
Of a riotous white in bloom
tinged with longing,
a colour so primary
would make the air blush.
Or perhaps nothing like that.
How would I know?
There I lay
patted now and then

by a dry blade of grass,
sniffed at and kicked by the foxes,
hugged in the warmth of bulrushes'
lap, thrown off by the hard winds
to lick the salts of soil
and grow a nose for them.
I could see with this
one spot in the head
whose full-sized blackness
is an apology for an eye.
And lying there I began
to hear things,
the whispers of the plants,
birdshriek or tattle.
And the pesky insects, for which I
sometimes wished I had the right snout,
and probably got one.
And the resonance of stones.
How smoothly the reeds in the stream grew
vertically aspirant.
Anyway, where I am now
I cannot get much carried away,
no more.
It was blustery that day,
with the westering sun nearly at edge.
The light but palpable steps
came nearer
the spot of ground which held me so
I would not quite belong to it or grow;
a dried up something,
wattle sheared, off.
A grasping hand lifted me

and then put me on a cold shelf,
metal, like wood or stone,
but polished, in somebody's home,
indifferent, amidst the bric-à-brac
of collectibles over the seasons;
family photos, souvenirs, trophies
of those whom I think to be people,
who have got themselves a life
like the greeting cards next to me,
with roses hand-painted.
Yes, I have developed an eye
and an ear for them
so I can will this few inches of body
to believe
what they say about themselves.
And I have even a leg to stand on,
for the front and the back each;
and partly lean against a family
photograph to stabilize my posture.
The body appears to be complete
from the only side seen,
and I have a roguish tail
for the behind
to swish off any doubts or flies.
The family is almost proud of me;
I am fondly introduced to the guests
as if this were my lineage,
as a natural avatar
of what in this world is called Desire.
They call me Howinteresting,
or Nice for short,
the name nicked in their tongue.

Alas, I have been accustomed here,
like all else, to being me.
As I heard of the Eid moon sighted
the other day, the crackers
and sparkler of joy going off
in all directions,
I just could not help it;
it shot forth from my throat,
this cry.
I had lived up to it thus far,
whatever was expected of me,
quiet to the quietest degree
of acceptance. What now
as they cry wolf? What now?
It was that particular tone,
the sadness, the lostness of the howl
gave me away.
They know it's another kind,
which they know other things to do with.
God knows what's on their mind.

Note: A.S. Babar Hashmi, ambassador, friend of the arts

SALAAM TO TS'AI LUN

See,
before he boiled it
and rolled its pulp into thin sheets,
this bamboo was the book –
handy, vertical, quilled –
in Chinese.

Had to be returned to the library
in an ox-cart;
your hand hugging as if a baroque tree
that you would see
and admire without climbing.

Reader, don't take this book to bed.
It will take your sleep away.
Half-timbered,
the fillings and joints of thin gatherings
interleave the earth and the heaven.
Its lips are sealed with gum.
And the words glow warm as flesh
as you shudder at the thought.

Note: Ts'ai Lun, c. 62-121 AD, patron saint of modern papermaking

LINE RENT

goes up
and down with time,
the stopwatch in someone else's hand.
All there is
is a little space to fiddle with.
To cut the long story
(that everyone knows)
short,
one turn of phrase
rears talk.
Heard syllabic?

Suppress the content
(for police' sake)
and (dammit) the tone
gives it away:
how your voice
still has not learnt
to tackle urgency!

A conversation
would be surfing, and all-expenses,
in Costa Brava.
Did your dad
or anyone else
ever agree to that?

You may get by
without it, in London or Paris

or another bush of your choice.
But here is the deed.
No matter how you
budget your words
day after day
minute by minute,
it's plush with numbers,
always due.

THE CITY NOT BEING US

We live in you
because you are not us –
and are thus
our only hope, true
to the waking dream
of how it could be.
The tang of rubber or plastic
burning in your alleys,
the smear in certain parts,
leafy green brushed aside,
birdsong called to a halt
 – screeching,
from these we can tell it's you
from how you could be.
Rain is not wet,
a hesitation clouded over.
And it's too long to the monsoon
for a yearly bath.
However brilliant this form,
your shadow, mark,
slips through the fingers, ever dark,
but not your charm.
We lick you fresh
upon each nightfall.
The tongue prints your body
with what meaning we can give you;
each word, oozing, or tear
claims a likeness or hue
and calls
to that handful of happiness:
you.

IN PRAISE OF LINSEED

Spared by the oil-press
it has even
survived people,

although they eat it
like animals.
It is cake

and ale
by turns,
painting non-crack

the insides
of your stomach.
So a capsule daily

may agree
with you.
Smooth to the end,

it remains elliptical:
little feeling, yet
is sticky with wet.

LINSEED: AN ANNIVERSARY

Sir Lancelot hardly knew
    or he would have gifted
    it to Guinevere.

No need of a belt,
    lock and key.

Just a marble
    pressed into the frog's throat.

No French.
    She had a taste for soda pop.

Each night
    the thirst would grow

big
    and propagate the same view.

That is what?
    Fuzz.

BAN

In Mururoa
there is a power to silence all
mutual confession and whispers,
kill the trade
in rumour, gossip, affection.
It's the blasts not heard
that people desert so early
the waterfront bars and the boa-
like ocean along the beach
that constricts them to these islands.

Where are the retired sea captains,
slouching planters, boatswains,
lawyers, bankers,
and pilots of vac aircraft?
The stunning Samoan blonde
just out of her bikini?
The schoolchildren diving
into the blue lagoon
from the bows of a vessel from Vanuatu?

How is one to loosen up the serious
boondoggle of species from afar?
First, Bougainville stopped off for a bite
and tagged his name on to our flowers.
His men hooked us to their skirting faith
and, as if in return, gifted us
Europe's venerable disease.
They all came, one after another,
in their sloops, looking for such a paradise

where one could dream before nature,
dot or space time to a line
or crumple it for the corner basket.
And here it was: in Hiva Oa or Tahiti,
off the steamer, Gauguin painting, happy
suckling at the mangoes
for inspiration, tree after tree.
And ready victuals:
breadfruit, absinthe or claret, women.

Now the earth implodes
I don't know how many thousand
leagues below the sea.
No upward mushroom
to delimit the heavens –
for that is done already;
just the invisible downward kill.

If the earth shakes
with muted rage
or the sediment is a shine faster
or darker, it's just the water's concern,
whatever, whoever, wherever breaks.

Tuna, Mahimahi, Wahoo –
all know it in their bones
and in the fission of their body
clung to the coral,
weedy raft of the testy sea.
Foodchain like them,
I do not like
to eat lead or mercury.

Here again the slow current
from the atoll caresses the island,
a Pacific gesture to the strand:
This French kiss is without radiation!
But has anyone asked the Shellfish?

These flowers, they blossom and blush
into so many colours all over
looking for their name.
No, my soul was not annealed
for your dyestuff when you last came.
My earlier wounds have not healed.
Please bring me no further civilization.

N.B.

It was not being averse
to the town.
Just that the smokescreens
it threw up the customary blue

became thicker & thicker,
and the birds in their pinks or greens
of roadside leafage
were hard put to it:

birdsong,
something to turn over a new leaf;
ever fit to rehearse
the twitter of time past –

an open-and-shut case.
The red-vented ones
had the face
to pass for a nightingale.

No speaking terms with the horizon.
Dust filled the air.
The poets sang, yes,
to their own boutonnière.

But the river was the one
constancy it knew,
circling its waist
to the baritone bend.

The sandman sitting like a camp-stool;
midnight mumblings of the water;
a little light from the far house.
What else?

Someone must have lived there.
One October,
the wind did go nipping through the alley;
shop awnings away.

Broken orange tea
mixed with betel
leached into the ears
beep-beep:

the hottest ghazal
of the day.
Needn't have seen
the heads sway.

ARRIVAL

It's hanging gardens from the town below.
Up there, a good jeep drive
as I speak with a friend:
the travois and dogs I had in the North
have life insurance now in museums,
and I don't.
Richard Wright hasn't been here?
Blackboy stands his ground
even this other side of the mound
next to his favourite bush;
a middling tree that is
free of leaf, branch, even roots
it seems – lives on air and light.
From something taller and rough yonder,
a kookaburra shouts what might
be a laugh,
chopping the park
and its livelong day into a half.

Our y-turn leads to Perth,
bathing in the last sun.
She tells the Swan
to flow on for another sixty miles
(or perhaps minutes)
before the ocean reclaims the earth.

SUGGESTION

Everyone knows
 – the old gardener posts
Keep Off –
here
love-lies-bleeding.

The sun sets
in the wisteria,
a hundred points of light
within, before the grey descends,
birdsounds take over.

Late, though not too late,
about forms of such love
to hand; grateful.
May as well sublimate
with the lady-of-the-night.

THERE

The sun looks through
the three-cornered kite
above the houses.
It's ochre
against the litmus of desire;
sharp air the string.
I fly this scarlet every day.

IN ICELAND

The sweetest flower that blows
here, I say.

She gives me the lip, knows
I would kiss, if I may,

the utterance, its warm complaint
perhaps stopped midway.

She shows me a faint
purple where she earlier wore pink.

A rose is still a rose,
anycolour, anyway,

or so I came to think
of this petal against the frayed

edge of the twilit wind.
And there it goes!

SUMMER IS HERE

Summer is here
with its evidence
of migratory birds alighting nearby
to pick from the grasses
and water. The old housewife,
whom I haven't seen for months
in this street,
darts out of doors at the first thin
ray of the sun, adjusts her glasses,
and gets to weeding. She appears sure
her flower patch
awaits her smoothing hand, there.
I walk by like the last season,
and whether you know it or not,
I too had waited for change.
So that the line between light and dark
is ever finer, and daily
promises cannot be undone by the night.
What is likely was perhaps
always present but is within sight
here at this moment.
The sky's colour is not in question –
it's your eyes I look into.
There is a stillness of the deep
in that look.
The body's memory skips
details but that it feels for;
your hand is warm to my hand.
You say, I still care for you.

I fear people talk and traffic
drive away the words
we live on.
I want the air to form its lips.

LAURA

She had a crack-up right in the middle
of it all but said
it was no matter, really.
Other people had managed with it.
Still everyone talked about it
like the newspaper jitters
or the geologist's map of Iceland,
spliced with lava,
cold enough to touch.
She wrapped me around herself –
cashmere for a season.
Come May,
she swayed in the wind,
    a late Easter lily
by the steps of happenstance
or listless messages from the sea.

NE PLUS ULTRA
    for Edwin

Guinevere slept at Raffles last night
and took her morning ride with me.
Even the larks knew they should soft-pedal
their routine and not wing aloft.

To the beach our pedicab flew,
across streets, shopping plazas,
blocks of flats, Galahad in the saddle.
Her sarong of onion-skin was the only sail up
to bring home to one the far horizon,

ie, until one weekend Sir Lancelot
came visiting. So choppy the sea!
The P&O's whistling through the long night!

Note: Edwin Thumboo (1933-), poet and scholar

'ANY IDEAS?'
for Ursula

you ask.
And no matter what I say
from pretty close to cotton-picking,

soon it will be a yarn –
no, a novel there.
You can spin it better

than any Jenny
and write the rawness of the deal
into something

worn with grace, another life.
Actually, such being the season,
I am into wool-gathering.

Why,
I could say it's December;
but no.

Was probably not
meant to be
but turned out so

that the involutions
of inference
were the only clue

to a stretchable blue
awning of a sky
one could pull

overhead
and feel the edging
of a possible subject.

And it poured down
sometimes,
the water took its shimmerings

from the grey and green hills,
viola and grasses
sweetened the air,

and people spoke of fine
or filly weather,
swinging their wishes

up a tricky rainbow;
or indeed earthquakes,
as in Iceland,

as if two giants in the deep
blotted out from memory
had turned over in their sleep;

such revolutions of the earth
and related lava
as escaped the few

pressure valves
without compunction,
one way or the other

put paid to the furious
deed accordingly;
all but with this view-

finder and hardly a thought
to grip the pen –
lest all came true.

Note: Ursula Bentley (1945-2004), novelist

BIRDS IN A TREE: AN ELEGY

Before they took wing
the legend was there.

They sat together (which
seemed like necking to some)
on this branch for a spring.
It was an old tree,

an oak, sans intention,
and free.

Come September, the air
goes nipping through the woods
instinct to the root,
keening.

Of a feather,
they chirped a while

and fell silent.
Up in the blue turning to look

at this vanishing sight,
the sunset gold of leaf-fall,

a tree
that is wood to a fault
yet live from its own convention.

OFF THE EXPRESSWAY

Take the dirt road down
and you see it soon,
your line of country.
Step after sore step,
is this where you wanted to be –
wild roses puckered up
along brick walls?
Children, barefoot,
have left behind a street
full of game prints,
in earth colours
no palmist but God
must be able to read.
Old Phlegm has audience.
Birds fly,
out the tree, the house,
whatever's nearby.

BEING THERE

I

Any seaman would tell you
they live – yes they do –
knee-deep in the water.
Before you can ask, whatever it is,
they have set sail.
Better go inland to know the olive
from the land,
its summer free as its tide.

II

I speak with Dante in the middle
of the night,
in the festive vernacular of winding streets,
about the actual:
breeze from the sea thrilling
to every return,
the tinkling of a distant bell.

We pause.
Two good men walk by wondering aloud,
and the one in frock-coat speaks American.

III

I have to postpone everything,
first boat or train out.

Later, someone speaks to me half-asleep.
She's analysed the sunflower for years:
Why look it?
Yellow hair plucked off the reggae
every sixth or seventh day?

I only listen.
Wild pollination's future.
And Umbria's here to lip
the latest promise under the sun, time.

SONNET AFTER THE TSUNAMI

Oh the sea will return and sing out
our names from the leagues below;
claim its face here –
nose to the horizon,
its lips of mud,
foaming eyes.

Pa and Ma are in the heavens.
They are safe. Neighbours and
animals gone,
birds so quiet what's speech
for? A throaty sound of this
one pebble on the beach.

Roll it again,
roll.

ABOVE BALAKOT

Split the trunks of trees;
the chenar, the walnut, the pine,
all slain, lie in the rift.
Naked, roots sever from the flesh
of this dark earth.
Holler! Valley and Mountain!
They must call each other by new names.
Exchange what is left; but not a sound.
If any people lived here,
they are gone, quiet to a fault.
For them, the rumbling down below
is over. The winter solstice may not return,
the snowfall cease.

IT WAS QUAKING-GRASS AWHILE

It was quaking-grass awhile
and hearing it breathe
like an old man, wheezy,
through the snooze,
kept me dreaming
about a bit of fluff
gathering to sing
in the moors of Yorkshire.

Then it shook a leg,
rhythmic ground.
Awake now, I saw my house tilt
to a side,
then spring back
aright beam and column
and hard brick
inside the quirky plaster
of this moment.
The windows are still chattering.

This house will probably
dance through the night.
And I too,
in and out every now and then,
with it; will not let me sleep.

My friends hear the castañetas
round the corner, a form of ancient art
they know the place
will give way for, any new start.

NEW ORLEANS, 2005

Drained
of voice,
even need,
it's secure
as the sea
it now makes peace with.

Sure runs in the blue veins
of those gone –
elsewhere.
The same magnolia blossoms
around Evangeline.
At her side drops a pintail.

Its still eye
pictures Venice by default.
No jazz
for the Duke,
what with the croaking
of politicians.

All cities are returned
to the land
like Atlantis.
No heir is untrue.
She will take us all in
again: me, even him, you.

Note: Lines written in witness of the aftermath of Katrina, a hurricane that destroyed the US city

EARTHWORMS

Those crawly things, the slime?

Razzle of random falling
rain in sectors the forecast failed.
That is monsoon.

But the earth has formed them,
nurtured for this day,
released.

Off with your wellingtons,
let them go.
Smell the earth's moisture.

They slither, slide, copulate, or recoil
from any outline drawn here,
assuming life, and hardly know.

SISTER CITIES
Written upon watching ceremonies in *This* and *That*

The mayors have declared them sister cities
and now admonish the lot about incest,
withholding visas, buoying the currencies.
Your fingerprint is found on her eye-test.
Who named these a family – Sodom and Gomorrah?
Such choice from the less to more of a
prison must of course be officially blessed.
No wonder the people of Lesbos object
to how the folk screw up their relation,
their name, to do their preference, elect.

NO END TO SUMMER

Why belittle this summer's call,
the trumpet-vine's soft orange intent?
It infuses the air with responses.
Outer wall's a honeysuckle blasé, in scent.

O yes the warmth. In this original garden
she doffs what she wears, helps unbutton mine.
Nature has little else to do.
Everything is in line.

BETWEEN THE RIVERS

So many had dived for that one anemone
at the river's final drop. And there!
That rare flower by the sea.

Who would bring it so far up to the lee?
What's the name of this withered branch,
ah, in the dying wind?

Mesopotamia, Mesopotamia.
Plucked from home,
must turn a leaf, swap memory:
rich river valleys with orchards
and a date-palm ripening at the edge
of the world.

Embarras de choix?
Those clear-eyed men and women figure out
bloodlines that crisscross into the plains
from every mountain slope.
Night is a whisper under the morning star.

Now up and about their daily chores,
working the land.
Out the toxic growths of years of despots.
So rough the step east,
all re-set the watches, have another business.

They are ploughing again,
demining country for their children.
Here they come
an unlikely spot,
tut-tutting.

Driving their cattle and themselves
with some hoo-ha about
sowing foreign grain in the land.

TO A QUERY

No, a quake,
downside
up to vibrations
that tell apart
the yard maple
from its bark,
inside being outside, see
that shag of brown grass
perhaps an old man's beard
show through the dirt
still hiding school children
from lessons in life sciences
whose last slowing calls
seize the essence of the matter
inside this earth
as it shakes
free of her burdens,
life races past
all attachments,
leaving you
oh but where

THE CITY WITHOUT FOOTPATHS

The city without footpaths
is one for skywalking
in the coy glimmer of star routes.
So many tracks under these lights here
that one may not take at the same time,
switching will take another life, and to make up
for scrabble is offered a juicy postscript;
the same turning for a pitch one thought
was known – but the toes hit
the lumpy edge of a rathole.
It too belongs to the base.
What's that ground to grab your feet?
Only a step back and the apple blossoms,
earnest of season perhaps or due,
light up the distance, over there.

'STARS TO GRIEVE AT PAVAROTTI FUNERAL'
Reuters, 8 September 2007

This sky above knows kindness,
will be raining tearful,
and those twinkling things up there too
have a heart, it is good to know.
Down here, even the brightest one
has gone to dust.
Watch that bowl of time
swell from the ground
tasting the ashen lip;
hands almost holding
what they feel to be there.

BEDS IN THE EAST

were bare charpoys and so many
years of bruised knees
in knotty relationships,

but across the seven seas
the prairie's emptiness
had another end.

Once she rose from the ground,
forward, her blue eyes turned brown
the deeper he looked into them.

No, no fourposter; no drapes.
Her hair's good twine.
She wanted him to pull at it twice

during the day and the night,
to ride out the storms Midwest:
hey, be tight, warm, nice.

WOODPECKERS

Their flight paths are hardly known
but they first alight on the house wall,
then the wooden railing, and one by one
step up to the outer door of my father's
room; knock, knock, knock.
One of them turns around, flies back
up the wall. The other one,
just the same restless stripe –
a warm brown, grey, black-white –
gets back the same tapping sound
from the shut door – peck, peck, peck,
skilling patience to flying
an angle of possible sight.
The third watches
through the rush of this moment
set deep in the wall,
his eye amused, his feathers aflutter.
Meanwhile, these two look at each other
and the door with no one in view,
fly into the next guava tree
by the look-alike house door,
its answering silence, or perhaps more.

COMPOSITION IN EARLY WINTER

On this frequency
though sound is clear,
sense agitates.

Familiar birds
wear foreign names
and intone their signals

in failing October light.
Leaf by leaf,
the summer signs off.

I can not help it all.
What is to fall now
will fall.

NOW, NOW

If you look up the map,
the terrain fails the plumb-rule
with its charm, green paper
stacked up the totem-pole.
Petiolar life, as long as
there is something else to speak of.
Not buildings. Yes, buildings.
Built for outages.
Tomorrow to bomb shelters
and bread-crumbs of yesterday.
Dark hissing wind and hail warn you
this morning about all that will pass,
allowing a sliver of light;
one magnolia blossom
sways over the sun-roof –
that awakening fragrance,
the years gone by.

CAMP OFFICE

Prayers were answered
with little rain
but that naughty bird
sent it down
pat on my forehead
if it wasn't for the windshield.
It runs to all sides and hardens
in your face –
lacquer it would not take.
Not that I wanted my peacap to hang
at home, on a brass hook,
whose very shape
cocks a snook
at everything up there.
In any case I need good wipers
before I land in office
and speak with club mates
on the flying bird-part
and a sanctuary for
what's equally endangered.
Go – try as you may
 – see for yourself there,
and there, and there.

COMPOSITION IN EARLY SUMMER

The last cactus in the burning sun,
and the air sucking
O the promised spit of land.

This dark fistful of pumice-stone
is a treasure; sinuate shores touching,
the desert scales off.

Where are those words – I've
heard good and strange,
shiftshapes of desire?

Again the tail of language
wagging
like a shadow of time.

Waters name this place;
go, go round it
for that vein.

FIRST INFORMATION

I

I take the police inspector around the house
and show him how the crimson Virginia creepers
and what remains of fruit trees in the backyard –
loquat, mulberry, guava
raised in good decades –
have been hacked and torched by miscreants.
The boxwood hedge and the lawn have been turned
to ashes. It's not the first time.
I have reported awful incidents before –
a break-in, a robbery,
and a threat to kill the family.
In all this he sees increasing crime
staring at the trees still here
 – the apricot in flower, stand-alone lime,
and assures a full investigation this time.
The butterflies and sparrows that come here daily
for sap or seeds and shade are now hasty visitors.

II

The next day I drive to the police station
to pick up a copy of the First Information Report.
The ditch in the middle of the road yawns;
wants to swallow me.
Now a big toad jumps atop
what looks like a gutter,
about eight inches above the road level;

opens its mouth for a full body tremolo.
I turn the wheel around; park aside
to take a look at what I can hardly face.
Inside, it looks like a clay oven
saved from Gandhara antiquaries.
Maybe it was used to bake your own bread.
But roaches swarm the place,
stealing food and water supplies in doggone odours.
Everything flows down here in other forms.
Praise this model management by roaches
in there, a fulsome colony
of cadre termites and silverfish
in the street, home, and forest, keen
and diligent through the under-cracks.

III

They scurry out of this rotting neighbourhood every dark hour
and change into anthros in baggy pantaloons:
upholstered, fanged, ever in office.

Nights, my sleep is riddled with bullet holes;
abrupt rounds fired from Mr Kalashnikov's zealous
rifle in bigoted hands. Who will give
a reason? O how to get past encroachments
into the civil terrain? Fresh body parts are sold
as scrap, and lamb's blood is daily spilled
in the street where you and I are trying to live.

IV

In the meantime, the car engine has overheated
and has to be turned off.
Give it fifteen minutes,
so that everybody can blow their horn at you.
You restart, reverse, and half circle around
to get to the next turning, at a mere 30 miles an hour.
Without a warning sign, you next hit
a speed breaker the size of the Great Wall.
Your head knocks into the car ceiling.
It's a speed bump,
yes, on your dear head.
The traffic warden shows his face in the muddle,
gives you a ticket – for being careless, sir, about your head.
You leave the car at the roadside
with emergency lights on, hail a taxi
and ask to be taken back to your house,
even as the trees and the flowers are all but gone.

NORTHERN VALLEYS

Three walls of the hutment
were fine as spring
caught the wild as a fire
we shut our eyes on.

Flowers sweetened the fields.
Fireflies sat pretty
on mushroom tops
hardly anyone picked,

before the iron tanks
rolled in.
The fourth wall,
not up yet,

let us out to safety
among strangers,
third-floor windows staring down
the half bare bodies,

baggy pants at street corners
shivering in the winter.
We were not to speak a word
about the earth that held us close

had the bayonet in her chest.
Move On,
the air shouted.
Next Herd!

'SLAIN WORKERS UNDAUNTED'

by risks, friends say,
as our best newspapers print
and emails confide
in well-guarded spaces
we still like to call our own.
They gave eye-care
in remote areas,
crossing a footpass
sixteen thousand feet above
life and a lungful of diseases
long forgotten.
Their local dialect slid off
the rocky trail.
Then they were out of breath,
could hardly see.
How does death rage in the hills,
not know a place too far?
Tell me more about fear
past the tonnes of snow
over their bodies
in Afghanistan.

RESCUE

It was one of those calls,
in the middle of the night,
to the number people are told
to save in their cellphones
if they can't learn by heart.

State workers look busy
in their uniforms and wear
a look in accordance
with the occasion.
They have almost cleared

the ground, and one of them
is doing the last bit possible:
swiping the pouring sky
on a rough
table-cloth found in the bin.

A check, red and white
blocks, for an alternate
view, and a later examination
by God knows who
of their earth-moving din.

Their eyes pretend
I am not there, and that's
all right. So much else is not
there, and has brought
no one to sight: irrelevance.

Tell me how to face
what was a clapboard house,
with children, their ma
in the kitchen making a meal for them,
their father away at his forester's beat.

AT EIGHTY-SIX

he died, they said,
the oldest elm in the park
brought up here by my mother
from down south,
where she saw a lone
young sapling in the wild.
Garden care was not for him,
but got used to the attitude;
the leaves tinkled every summer
and beckoned us children to play
or rest, timely embrace the comfort
given when no one else came along.
A week now, the dirt
and the remaining dried up roots
are cleared to make room
for whatever else is possible.
Ground's level, ever.

HOW PALE THE FIRST MOON OF THE YEAR

How pale the first moon of the year.
Your words, damp air of the unspoken,
or perhaps that same treacherous
ground beneath our feet
sliding in sheets of rain; this last killer landslide.

You say, weeks of mud; I agree.
Let someone else notice the coming numbness.

The cabin, sheltering the lost here,
now a pile of sticks or straws,
souls out of place, nowhere to fall.
At least the sky no longer sieves
through the roof.

Bird wings flapping somewhere,
within hearing distance,
a shriek pierces the dark snows.
Weren't we warned of the drifts,
passing touch of bodies, disturbed sleep?

Tracer lightning still rummages in the dark:
it's only a goat track winding through the hills,
going round and round. And then
an uneasy stop to rush through,
as only a leafless elm fends for itself.

How the naked roots clutch at the edge of a crag
in here, and here, and here.

It's not the roots; shortness of breath
sets off a riff
down the tremulous valley.

POST

The left hand pulls the cord
to allow in creaking transom light
so I can catch the last week
in post, at least reading
with my right.
Dark words in there –
folks killing each other
every sundown – print
their shadows on my eyes.
No return address.
The tea-table stays here as
the maypole of envelopes yellowing
to the floor tile.
Is this life I lay aside?
Do, please, write again
if anything is left there to see.

NOT MOVING

Look at it:
this park bench sits here
almost as I sit here, waiting not
to be disturbed by mendicant friars
and mullahs. Those continents
I quit. The world was big enough.
I still read some. The last fold
of the county map has some highlights
creased for tomorrow, a visitor's paradise
at first light – the lakeshore sanctuary
of birdwing sails spread in white –
before the day wears on,
the plum ripens to fall off the tree.

Smart bodies gleam past the upper edge
of the page, while their runner shoes
figure tracks into the smell of dust
rising.

Eye-glasses off.
Only to clear the speck
under which
the last continent has disappeared.

EAST RIVER

Across Carl Schurz Park,
beyond Hoop Garden sloping the other way,
is the river bank. Daylight,

I pick this walk through the dahlias,
trying to forget who fought here,
and when, to what purpose:

East River's among the most honest,

and impish, it flows in one direction mornings,
another for afternoons.
No source as such; just water at the ends.

I would like to be its temperament.
At six in the evening, children play ball
with their dog; a woman jogs far into the sunset.

JOSEPHUS' FOOTNOTE TO HISTORIA

All of Pharaoh's lean eastern kine
actually went down to dine
at the nearest 7-Eleven.
The chili sauce in straight and saline
hot dogs got them right
to Los Angeles the night
before they went up to Heaven.

TRYST

A grey metalled road had us circling
fast round sweet miles of forest,
groves of red cedar, tea-leaf sycamore,
even a hickory akimbo.

We couldn't wait for a bed of pine needles,
touch of velvet. Maybe the sun played
peek-a-boo through the branches.

A raven, our vocal witness,
cleared his throat once
and flew away.

We haven't carved our names
anywhere; *we'll come here again.*
There was no path in view:
we'll wend our way through here.

Lakeshore, in the afternoon,
you held my hand in the dinghy.
Warm waters sprayed in
as the sun made the current run strong.

The oars lay idling: *I won't let us sink.*
A week later, when I said
I have a sinking feeling,
you weren't there.

AMUSEMENTS FOR ELINOR WHITE

You can see everybody has been on a high
ever since I took the road less travelled by.
Gone to England, with a boy's will,
the birches all so rippling bright
and wet to touch did me good there
in every season, horse farm or hill.
Back in New England, future's reference,
they write as if all orchards had been laden
with passion fruit, picked regularly and
sold upmarket with a vengeance by those
comics in khakis or Goodwill tweeds
I would hire – without a ladder, bucket and clue
for such field practicals. They broke the garden
hose last summer, and now terrorize the trees.
I have lost some sleep over it, this my land,
as only somebody else, across the bush,
barely visible, has the lowdown on the weeds
that overrun the funky borders of desire.
Hear the voices of children poolside? The birds?
It is about the same all over, with this difference.

NUMBERS

It may be rational but hasn't overtaken
death, this counting of years gone by
or yet to come; that in B.C.,
they used to die of numbers decreasing,
just as the tide neaps for all,
all to a quiet harbour.

Talk of the time for them to swell:
nineteen ninety-nine, or so,
as all earth's waters meet above
its crepuscular motions
occluding the skies with countless stars.
Degrees of deathly waters rising.
Useless arithmetic.
They warned us
with needle eyes of lightning,
almost heard,
so that we would prepare ourselves.
Examples fall short
of this precise moment
wherein substance makes little sense
and even words perhaps cannot pass.
A recessional would be reasonable
for those here, around, hence.

There was talk of pound, shilling, pence,
circulation of blood lines across the tough
borders of sight, opinion about weather.
About life, what do I know?
Enough!

STILL LIFE
with Olga Khokhlova

Don't know why these are called Dole.
Bananas,
nonetheless. From the republics.
Blackholes we shunned long ago
titillate a particular old need;
suck like mangoes.
You and me they tear at, carve up, feed.
Actually the whole world is grinding
that missing bean for my cup of coffee.
This bunch is real nice yellow-green, long,
licking sweet as the weight of our mutual hunger.

Remember when they came dangling out of the blue?
Old Pablo juggled these in La Paris,
ones or twos, though not for me,
while you split yours in Pakistan.

Forget the price tag, baby.
We'll settle that later.
Come on, peel.

Note: Olga Khokhlova (1891-1955), Pablo Picasso's muse and first wife

HAPPENINGS

Her mother remembers how in the end
she died of third-degree burns from a kitchen fire,
and she can't get over it, the cup of tea
her daughter made her every day
remains empty, with her gone under tonnes
of earth. Then, her brother shot in the head
by state agents for being a nice guy
not helping street crime. So many years ago,
blood soaked through the clothes he wore,
the clothes stolen by thieves who could not tell
the old wash from the new,
but the wound right there festers.
The neighbours' boy hurt in crossfire
between vigilantes is still lying in hospital,
comatose. His father received his report card
from school the other day,
keeping the position to himself,
and retired to his room.
He said to his wife it was only junk mail.
Not seen for days on their lawn;
their curtains are always drawn.
Another heartache,
one that kills neat.
That bomb last week, some eighty splattered
in the bazaar, shopping for clothes, homewares.
The roadsides explode every day,
intention given to dynamite.
Ambulance service has a backlog,
and no one answers a phone call:

ma'am, please wait, goodbye, if at all.
Who can tell these folk
which terror they have been spared?
If you look for the truth or dare say why,
you'll be gone before you can ask.
She sinks in her easy chair breathless,
morning paper on arm rest, trying to read.
She knows hearsay is as good as life:
for death is on the prowl,
meeting us day after day
so we can learn its fine pseudonyms.
Then she looks out the window
into the person-filled street.
Black cars, hearses, pass by as usual, zigzag.

PEONIES

Now that the garden has been bulldozed
by local managers, the jasmine
has been put to the ground for now,
lest the man in Burgstrasse 19 admire
the scent he feels coming through
the clear window across the seas.
Done with gardenia, I toyed a while
with black-eyed susan (even drank it
dry in Kentucky), so that every other year
all would appear to come back alive
while she died, and I died with her.
This current patch of clay, now sand
or rocky ground, is one I thought
had a natural course for care, a furrow
deep enough in time for other flowers.
So I worked this land from end to end,
but they have taken away the light,
shade, good rain, even the earth for them.
I raised all from a nursery, the peonies,
this bright, lovely buckeye belle
that no one may buy, no one may sell,
a song that I hear day and night.
Anyway, it's in my ear. You might have a
use for perennials, so I send you these.

GOD SAID, LET THERE BE AN END

God said, Let there be an end
to this nonsense: they can eat their Galas
or what they want elsewhere;
they can't even resist themselves,
spare fruit, grain, drink;
can't speak a word
until it's put into the mouth.
Let them have their do.
This is not the place for them,
crybabies crèche, kindergarten
to college on roller skates
so they can pay rent and utilities,
fall sick working or not-working,
make and clash swords to draw blood
for more and more – tastes of the flesh.
They will resign later to salads
of puritanical diet, resort to confessions,
look for a deal past the funeral rites.
Now let them make up their own stories.

They crossed that invisible threshold
to outer space together, she first.
All they had or knew was hunger.
Where were they?

Two vicars came by, much later,
to hand them brochures they could not read.
So one's oral directions were for Macy's
to get some clothes before the other
pictured for them Campbell's soup
and vendibles they could afford
from their social security pay.
The vicars, their son and daughter down the line,
hardly knew these strangers from abroad.

They may have lived or passed through life,
be still around, with us, we haven't a way to know.
Death was a house chore, avoidable.
Now it lives just across from here,
has an address.

ENLISTED

first for a cause and pepped up by medals
now I forget the reasons that got me here.
The hands waving good-bye to the ship
leaving the harbour were sad. How quick
tears in your palm dried with the sea wind.
Enough rounds and rations; the choppers,
GPS, night vision – all gizmos working the front
to make grass widows of countless women
in foreign jungles. Anyway, I write
to you briefly from my mosquito net,
under the passing search beam
as Sarge snoring next to me sleeps tight
and cicadas drone on like him at group meets.
Anyway, we do as we're told. Take care,
I must be up early and help whoever fights
for peace around, speaking of equal rights.

OCCASION

He's gone, the voice says.
Before I can ask where to,
the call disconnects.

I find him sleeping peacefully
through the ride on old city roads,
the crowd's whisper about what happened
towards the end.
Flowers and faces morose,
they appear at his side and disappear.
His limbs are stiff.
The eulogy distracts all for a moment –
he'll be safe and well some place else.
Before he travels again,
so many hands touch each other
trying to grasp the moment:
there's a silence,
but no looking away from nervous
thin legs of the bier,
ground softened from long slow rain.

The earth's dug up every time it happens
as a way out of here.

Someone says we're running out of land,
they are going.

So where are we to meet next?

RIVER POEM

She is sitting cross-legged
in the grasses at the banks of the Great River
and writing again,
pulling Mister Johnson out of the depths
perhaps no one has fathomed before.
She knows the name is not Niger.
The blue ink pen glad in running hand
across the page is used to her hold,
manner of thought, left-to-right,
the indigo alphabet of his and her will.
She has heard that somewhere
a sea-stretch away they call it black.
Pekuah passes by, barefoot
in her pantaloons and shama.
She is already speaking to the stars
that will come on tonight;
all about Nekayah and perhaps
a meeting if not happiness of sorts.
An angler nearby hasn't said a word
since morning; no catch.
All he says now is I have this dress
for you to conceal nothing,
though it's not foreign.
He thinks she is hard of hearing
and goes away muttering
Mistah Kurtz – he not fully dead.
It's fun people she is writing about,
regardless; they are who they are.
She knows the moment,
the lie of the land,

the name of each blood drop
coursing through its veins.
Her writing is the colour of water
all earth takes.
Underbrush or plenitude,
she is finishing this full chapter
and will soon break for lunch.
Suddenly, a large trunkfish
jumps out of water
and lands on the last paragraph,
slippery wet,
not blinking an eye,
word shapes heaving
under shifting weights
of the piscary.
It's this that matters now
pulling at the line, strung up
inside the turning seas,
and an egg sinker
in the river mouth
that can not hold water.

CROSSING THE ALPS

Sort of placed here, yes, he remembers
being with you at some point
over there, crossing the borders and guards
whose vanity box has just one secret:
Keep Them Apart.

He found a way around it, froze
in the landscape, local twang and weather,
kissing you to snows relenting,
gaining time. But the sun forever slid off the Alps.
That snowman has since migrated

to regions he'd better keep to himself,
for their sake, for life needs saving;
its rigid grace invites the sun-spots
to his face; cyclones, random cloudburst
in tropical streets winding back after all

to a sensible grove, the bending bough of seasons.
Thus he chose what he chose, credulous to a fault.
Just as the bluebells work heads down even here
as fancy streetlights. Facing these again
he tastes melting flakes, your salty letters.

ALL TOO OFTEN A GREY BOULDER ROLLS DOWN

All too often a grey boulder rolls down
over me. Ends the hike to fresh springs.
I must push it aside with my bare hands
or it sits on my chest day after day –

grey lump in my throat.
Hard-pressed to test my voice on the rough hillside –
the murmur echoes back
from the valley, fields, catacombs of waste.

Another tremor, it sets me free.
The sky is a cleft in the range for now.
A thin blue stream gurgles through seasonally.
It feeds the village pond

where the sun warms our daub house.
A week of landslides and rock falling on rock
tells Gaia the weather gods are stone deaf.
Waters only foam over it; then change course,

cut into the wait for yellow barley.
The waterwheel is still going round
down the track, and women hurry
to fill their earthen pots,

dunes loping across the line of sight,
a bucket full of emptiness.
O how the elements change:
the bottom falls out so there's no measure of dearth,

even as the winter sun comes on
to cancel the cold winds
and the sky stops
pouring.

SPRING AT THE DOOR

I

Spring at the door
calling in half sleeves.
Asked in, it has turned away.
How it then appears is pointless.

Winter's snow still covers
every bough in the garden

refracting the sun –
the deep-white glare
of things made invisible.

These clothes I wear
may be the only season
passing.

II

Not Yet in the waiting world;
the light turns every now and then,
darkness is less shaded,
being inside helps.
Still, where are you?

III

All winter this tree, anonymous –
so long a death rehearsed at my window,
this morning has tips of green,

an inkling of time working
quietly on each wishful rumour. So
the apricot's already in bloom east,

where the blue drops down to sea level:
the air's free and half-notes pick up
at the instance of faraway swallows.

CITY, WEST

They flower in the sunlight
by Franciscan towers, centerfolds and real,
while Sunday papers and wild headlines
hit the doorstep cold.
Park out lazy and the pigeons will coo.
Round every turn, the streets are waves
rising or falling to the horizon
you wanted to stroll into.
It's said the country's a deli,
poached fish and farm fresh avocados
which size up to your want.
Yet this city has called out for me:
loosen up the ropes – set sail to the insisting
blue in September,
hear out the frontier cello.

Day in, more light from portholes
above the Plimsoll line
of the creaky raft I must leave behind.
O what a fine jazz off the shore.
My apartment bobs in the sky.
Gulls and revellers feast all day,
go in and out
of an Ohlone chipotle.
So a private word – any psalm of the self
is caught mid-air by a diving sea bird,
ayed on the fly with a wink
as the breeze picks up.
Someone's paper hat was just blown off
across the ocean, perhaps to China.

It returns at night as full moon,
hung on the special branch
of an invisible tree
that grows without shade
or so much as an autumn leaf
sounding out the sidewalk.
It's then the sweet moonlight calls
and lovers climb up
the taking slopes of Pier Five.

The neon scroll in the market square
spells out Poseidon for next mayor,
the one ranching under water.
In any case, the great bridge
to cross over from the Pyramid
is only a few miles away.
If the ferry is a little late,
it takes all on the land free.
Listen to the wind from the sea,
walk straight on,
and though you don't see it right away,
the other end is equally heaven.

THEY SAY, THEY NEVER WROTE

They say, they never wrote
themselves – which gets my goat.
Fred Douglass espoused his secretary,
or *amanuensis*, when he became a judge.
She handled his long sentence deftly
and saved the bubbling fudge
for family occasions.
Another Earl of Rochester had a better ruse.
He rode and hunted by the day
and slipped into his English sleeping bag
at night, so tired he named the girl his Muse.
Maybe it's all made up by the scions
of pen-pushers wanting a rebate on the yarn,
and who have also made a go
at Zora and Phillis, right upto Olaudah,
abolishing them. Even easy-rider Du Bois.
For he may have hollered through the barn,
but to be read around ho, ho, ho,
W.E.B. double-bleached his memoir!

GARBAGE NEWS

> British Airways has shelved plan for a £340m project to produce aviation fuel from household waste.
> – Sky News (Thursday, 14 January 2016, 22:36 GMT)

I always knew
my garbage was pricier
than a generation fore and aft
and began to save
nearly all the bin stuff
God knows when –
perhaps since your previous call
for toffee wrappers, sneezing tissues,
batteries dying, used up time
in tired wall clocks,
round bottles with long necks
empty & inebriated,
burnt toast from late office-
breakfast, even my neighbour's
occasional throwback to modest
youth (sanitary towels)
so you refuel up there,
recycle the orbit,
or blip
off the bleak, eccentric skies.
Gravity's got us down here,
nose to the grindstone, slow
as the earth mocks
going round the night to day
to night as if
the rest reversed any less.
Oh, it was just for you.

Heading off counting to zero
nothing's going to fly.
Heap's piling up here,
now what shall I do?

FACTS

Well, we had lunch together
in a holiday restaurant that day
and recalled how long it had been
since we watched Louis de Funès
make a love-nest of his car
sliding from a rock
onto the slender branches of a tree
that was shaking to the roots
with him and her smooching and stuck
in its hair. Forget the gendarmerie,
but it wasn't called *The Cliffhanger*
or *Hampered and Hived Together*
even in sub-titles; and no real plot
except the derring-dos
and honest skylarking,
the fun of it all cherry-topped
with the blushing ripeness of ready fruit.
We laughed over good broccoli soup.
He cleaned the corner of his mouth
with a white cloth napkin.
Two men in plain clothes came by.
One tapped on his shoulder.
They took him away,
the last anyone's seen of him.
We just wanted a light meal
with a mousse finale.
The bulletins say
the old film buff disappeared.
His family keeps his room tidy,
his clothes nicely pressed

like certainties folded to be worn later,
expecting he'd walk in any day.
I have saved the stained napkin,
though somebody nameless
calls me every week
to hand over or else.

ADAM'S PEAK

Going along a loopy trail,
hours like days of walking uphill.
Gravigrades do it better.

Try a quick step in the narrow pass,
and it says: DO NOT GO OVER THE EDGE.
Step back, *back, back*, echoes the valley.
A thrill barely missed.

The final climb makes a minute
of the years it has taken me to get here.
I must stop a while to catch my breath.
The gravel crunching under my boots
almost threw me.
Air's light, the body hot as a potter's kiln,
fired up, wisping away.

 And then? is a question others too
have carried this far up the rise of earth.
For this figure out of all that's heard
on the way, a sure footprint,
a departure?
Between the heaven and earth,
only a certain shape of stone makes sense,
its fine-cut toenails tickling the flesh
of my hands.

No one has stayed here for long;
it's only the beginning of descent –

to an aroma of tea gardens,
all the way down to the villages
of elephant men, coconut women.
I should train to look again
on breathing undulations of the land
where the sun flashes its sequins
from a blouse of green.
Every summer break, in my sleep,
the same pulsars beckon in the dark.

Note: Adam's Peak is a place name in Sri Lanka. The legend says Adam landed on the earth here. A Buddha relic on the top of a mountain enshrines another memory.

EVERYDAY

Morning takes over the night
setting the clocks
to cockerel crow.
A broom sweeps the porch,
dust settling
particle by slow particle
so I have to sneeze
without a hanky.
An old woman passing by says
bless you,
though I tell her it wasn't
the god particle, thanks.
She looks back as if it were me.
Then the milkman knocks at the door –
two bottles of milk and a bill.
Off he goes with some extra coins.
His mule neighs to sentiment,
ears twitch as shifting sunlight
as late autumn clip-clops
out the house gate.

Far side trees lining up, a dirt road
lurches along,
then shivers back into the horizon,
and the trolley bell rings through the gaps.

If I have missed anything
in the fading air of late-late morning,
say breakfast for a clean wicket,
early birds have already
reported to the sky.

SO WELCOME, FUZZY WINTER LIGHT

So welcome, fuzzy winter light,
to this dark shed,
where the first sunrays fall through the pane,
the skylight over my desk –
and pour into the flower vase.
See, what gave out a fragrance
last night? Tuberoses splayed out asleep
or perhaps awakened late.

This hour is a window curtain swooshed
open to another view: right below the loggia,
turbo wheels roll out the lapping quick tarmac,
glass door entrances schooled to auto welcome.
Siderow plum seedlings stopped in their tracks.
Flowers we knew could timely blossom
in deed with us are pressed in books.
Azaleas, last, war-sick, crimson.

That metalled place has hissing lanes
made over the old park and quiet wooden bench
warmed then long into the night.
Remember white house doors, walls
in limewash whirl about on the bike,
the hurry to pedal out distances
through cold streets and just a moment
to lean on the curb for a last chestnut

before the barrow boy moved on?
The sky is still in place.
All may shut down but this light is free,
baring faraway tree shapes to sight.
It's not turned off by anyone
from lack – brinkline shifts further on;
the streaking blue flushed with yellow ribbons
thinning out the pinks and purples for a certain gold.

CONVERSATION

How nice the party this last day of the year,
and the resolutions. He sits down at his desk
now staring at a piece of paper, blank.
She walks in, mutters something, je ne sais quoi,
as if a dream had no ending.
And drawing a pencil line across
the page, indents it with a fingernail,
says this is where you live, right below,
at some angle of what you call choice, East Doldrums;
while she is above the tilt
made by her doodling hand,
a kind of horizon that any colour
on a white sheet could serve for,
say a livid lamp shade over Arctic light.
But how do you know where you live,
he says, West Doldrums? Horse Latitudes?
I know because I know is the only part spoken.
It sounds like 180° flat. A bruise in B minor.
He doesn't know what kind of line it is,
unhooked from verticals,
not seen in any map, or the palm of his hand.
She says she may not cross it
and he shouldn't either,
for the space is a wanting belly to lose yourself in;
would be packed as a silo
were he not such a square peg
and made her the first squiggle
of New Year worth his ink.
So he fumbles for the foot rule, protractor,

indiarubber for exacting care,
the compass and divider in his old school geometry box.
He too knows some things are missing
at the moment, above or below,
whichever's the name,
and he tells her sometimes,
scrawl or string as short as this.
Perhaps it is not visible to the naked eye.
He would not erase it though;
it's the only line keeps them talking.

FEST

of course we broke
the wishbone together
grip tighter with each twist
hands in the feel
of breaking even
plus thumb joint pressure
and feathers plucked
one after another and another
until endings of alphabet
her blue grass skirt rustling
in wicked sea wind
so we touch off the surface
light, sail easy
mix food with prayer
though we've gone
our own ways since
I holding up my end
of what looks like a stick
(no no no I have no
bone to pick
with anybody anything)
without knowing why
after such a fine meal
we made of it all
with cranberry sauce
at each port of call
on our this-world tour
up here or down under
swift bow and stern waves
hardly a tossup

but nothing to hear in the wake
oh the afterlife
of the poor wild goose
stuffed then
and done with smoothly
along three saints
and still every year
she texts me
happy thanksgiving

WHAT DO YOU KNOW?

My colleague, the archaeologist,
has dug out from flat earth
some cracked wood,
likely a piece of a tabletop.
A smear of soup or blood
within the crack and dirt
speaks to a time
she's carbon dating to bombs
hitting the place right.
No other witnesses,
I believe her.
She smiles and turns to me
with a steady gaze:
here it is, old Syrian,
the chance to go home.

YOUR DAD

Your dad died
last night, you told me
and you cried
silently into the phone.

I could only say I was sorry.
You probably had a lifetime
of love and more to do without.
He and I had been friends

for at least half that.
Fading skies for a week already,
there is no sunset to wait for.
My umbrella

upends a hollow in the dark
where it is still damp
and cold.
For him though the rain stops.

SIDES

Champlain is calm at sundown, so lovely
its shimmerings I can not fall asleep.
A bleb of air in winter floes, I breathe

from it for months. Summers, the air
lifts off the water, my place in crested
cottonwoods and green rocks rolling

as daylight. And the earth too changes,
a dab of colours in the wild. Clear-lined,
this land remembers how the old white sail

went up in the sky, or water reconnects.
Fish wouldn't have to make up their mind.
I might swim the bottled sea of Fundy.

BULRUSHES, NORMANDY

Though the sea washes up here,
ankle-deep, they are thoughtful,
and a league away in the waters
baby fish knock for help,

hide or slip away.
Evenings along the hedgerow,
in our house the rabbit's
warm in morels, wild flowers,
swigs of calvados. Sleep comes

fitfully like impromptu love songs.
But the days are nothing.
Strong current, it sweeps over
the lame fringe of brown grass
so the algae disappear

like birds in the sky –
from gun smoke drifting, hunters,
or wounds hurting just as yesterday.

Barefoot, this cold skin of the land
has its toes in the water and deep runny sand.

S AGAIN

For once the forecast has been correct.
I speak to her across miles of rain
(this beautiful woman I've just met)
by telephone, and tell her in the main
that I like the fine lilt of her voice,
and would phone again, were it my choice.
She agrees but cannot see through the April shower
that the old apple tree here has its first flower.

Maybe I run into her again Saturday at the local store
shopping for meat, drinks, and ice-cream: ...
the newsrack's ready pulp! What's more,
fresh veggies by home delivery. The cookout closes
around 4pm ... And still a day left to dream
about how the deer sprint to breakfast on roses.

ODESVILLE

Floating wishing lanterns on village ponds
or waylaid in March,
I missed the spring. Cloudburst April
careered over the ranges;
the last avalanche tore through the TV weather map –
kicked the hills into dirt.
      Now, day-long, the sun
blasts all shades of green, makes birds
            fall out of trees, desire
        run out in rivulets of sweat,   evaporate.
Left out here, my days must burn across these plains
rolling off the rocky mounds of Jhelum,
each stumbling goat track through one strip of wheat.

The orchards here that were –
    once sheltered
lovers, losers, migrant fruit
and fruit-pickers,
or the last royal figure topiary, shrub, sleeping vine;
all too far away to temper the salts
so munition the groundnuts of Chakwal.

Shift hard gears and cross the dry riverbed.
The water buffalo
and horse carriage are gone, sucked
through the milk tube, kala cavalry.

    Rawalpindi taxi
mercifully broke down midway;
it was numberplated RIP 1406.

Five bump-free hours was a boon
        but the road bends many ways,
time worn as landfills,
    cracks in the concrete
lines of dumpy embankments.

Vague house lights or dim shops
look out of clouds of dust and smoke
laissez-faire, soot or mud raining down,
dark talc the town face.

Is anybody home?
Who are these helmeted gladiators
on motorbikes
swerving left and turning right
                        full tilt,
fuming in their maze?
No stray dogs flexing their tails,
petrol cars rev up on yellow,
then accelerate.

GROUSE

I last saw it preening as a blueberry
patch some other place, and gosh,
here it is now, this one,
amid trees of heaven,

riotous red hemlock, larch and fir.
Whisper spruce, and with hisses,
low whistles and clucks, the leaves
stir uneasy, so I can tell the feather,

chest spot, or band from the rest.
Foraging far in the pine country –
needles after green shoots – it has altered
again, melting into the landscape;

shelters easy with flamboyant sumac,
letting in the fast underbrush, loud spice.
Lush mountainside, seeds, berries, lake
waters fill this dusky hornbeak

no matter the brownish desert kin
daily bathes in the dust. And in the park today,
looking up into treetops, I may have
overstepped the peace, tubers

or dry branches crackling everywhere.
So it looks out of red eyes, sore –
sideways of its nervous coat
of shifting colours,

scampers on the touchy ground,
wings spread out once, twice, clapped shut,
and readies to take the forest along
crazy brusque in flight.

SWEET WATER ONLY

Last round of the lane, dusk falling
across the district,
he's back where he began after the morning prayer,
hangs up his skin on a nail in the hurting wall
and falls asleep on a straw mat.
Half that pulpit wall went down
one monsoon along with his father.
The back of the wall is still some use.
At least, the mosque has a water tap,
his filling station, and a rent-free foyer.
He dreams about his father's dim eyes
looking in the distance, his kindly face
the only hope that was; a mirage
ebbing white in the desert he's known
since he saw his mother crying
round an old cot.
Azan, and he's up again,
rubbing his eyes upon the same star above
that waits out the twilit hour.
Day's work is a half torn shirt,
sun burning a white strap into the shoulder,
water skin on the back.
So bent for his years,
some would think he's been praying
in obeisance to God too much.
Each time he fills up and pats it
with a gentle hand,
then a jolt that settles the weight in place.
The steer hide still smelling good,
with him and his father's sweat

soaking in for maybe a hundred years,
from before Elizabeth became Queen.
It's something to smell to believe. Go,
hobble from door to door and see the smiling eyes.
People are hardly wrong: 'Look,
he carries the Arabian Sea on his back.'
And he assures like a town crier:
Sweet water only!

VIRUS REGULATION
a sonnet sequence

I

You are lucky you have your masks,
nearly all your personal protective
equipment. And you have your
instructions. The virus protocol
is a complete code of life.
Use the Coronavirus App
on your [expletive] smart phone
before it puckers.
Value these precious
minutes of the lifetime SIM
now ululating for the occasion.
Of course, you will wash your hands
ever, but you will not wash
your hands off the world entirely.

II

Every one of you
is a unique touch-me-not.
Reports agree the virus, a novel
terrorist, is omnipresent;
nothing's out of its reach,
mineral or vegetable, animal or human.
Caught half way casting off
its uniform, it seemed to escape
from one spot, then from another,

leaving numbers and ghost towns
gasping for breath; yet it has stayed.
For this, we have no prophylactics,
only sticky prefabs, porous border walls.
Watch over your shoulder. Watch now.

III

Summer nights, at the rooftop,
the long hours are hardly long.
Eighteen this year, buxom,
she lies over me full weight
and pull of the earth beneath us,
sweating into the silence
and tiny drops of body scent we make.
Skin to skin, we exchange all.

I inch forward.
A swift current through the satin folds,
or ruffled as grass, she sighs.
O I am not supposed to do much –
less and less counting of stars.
None too soon, none too far.

IV

Touching folks is lethal.
Sanitize 24/7
and keep your sanity.
See no one, shake no hands.

Ask no one to coffee.
Dating is out,
though chatting via video link is OK,
and for G-7 parties, kosher.
Love without touching
is chemically pure, neat. (*Ah, Plato!*)
Weddings are banned.
Funerals are such a lazy dispatch.
Why stand on ceremony
for bodies on the redundancy list?

V

You will live while you will live
as a fleeting shadow
falling off a sliver of light
in your personal cave.
It's where the pulse slows down;
time drops into a black hole;
tomorrow differs
from death, from birth.

Now would the babies arrive immaculate,
pink? Not just you, he, she, they –
all in the republic may expect to have them
through good vibes.
Or the stork will do deliveries,
for the endgame is yet to be.

VI

A silly little place to lounge
out of time's domain you could enter
not knocking at the door,
stow knick-knacks and potted gardenias,
and maybe return to for refills,
an extra cup of coffee;
it's the one you fancied owning some day
as home to you,

but is farther than anything in sight.
Never the same, really,
needs dusting.
Even the shoe-rack yells every weekend
'where've you been so long?'
And that same door to leave again.

VII

To all ends and purposes, online,
you will be homeschooled.
Stem lessons, our workaday gospel,
will be flashed straight into the brain.
Your schoolmarm, Ms Touchbutton,
will take care of the procedure.
Ha! Math is so musical, you can strum off
a concerto of infinite fractions. This time
the translators will be starved to undo
Latin, Arabic, Aramaic or Hebrew.
In your pueblos and cramped tenements,

you have you and your rotor fix, the algorithm
to work and play in splendid isolation,
your new society.

VIII

Stay within your national bubble;
let no one puncture it.
Nearly everything else
is something else.
Such other kinds flock here!
If you want to know the weather,
check the stock market chart.
If you have other ideas,
it's past prayer time.
Beware all doors,
(save makeshift hospitals and morgues),
all possible doors, outlets, exits,
places of worship, parks, colleges,
have wired Yale locks.

IX

Warm bread from the oven,
your hands smell of dough,
baking, the science of hunger
or satisfaction. You only say
we are out of cinnamon,

just as yesterday.
Another mile to go for spring water,
more herbs, and nuts for the buns.

Year-round
it's been
ploughing or gathering,
prayers for good weather.
Is it this we live for?
One waiting, the other away.

X

Feel socked in?
Turn on your service laptop, full screen,
and take a good look at how the world was.
See how the purple and yellow crocuses
spread wild in the city's main squares?
Given the chance! No wallpaper,
it's the name of the fragrance
in real time.

And hear the birds
in the park over there, right off
the busy lane empty today?
So excited, the bluegreen longtails swing
into a corner of your view
before it goes dark. Hear now.

XI

So be it, so be it, I am sure.
I am sure, I am sure, so be it.
So be it, I am sure, so be it.
So be it, so be it, I am sure.
I am sure, I am sure, so be it.
So be it, I am sure, I am sure.
So be it, so be it, I am sure.
I am sure, so be it, so be it.
So be, so be, so be, so be, it.
I am, I am, I am, I am, sure.
So be it, so be, it, sure, I am.
I am sure, I am sure, so be it.
So be it, I am, I am, I am,
sure, sure, sure, sure, sure, sure, sure, sure, sure.

XII

In here, true angels in spacesuits will feed you manna-
o-salwa. The state's done up.
You will be watered round the clock
with the choicest drinks.
The houries will nurse
and please you,
even if all the fine perfumes
of Arabia will not sweeten
their smelly big feet.
You will activate or rest
in their caring celestial arms;

and in good time
with their beguiling charms
they will lovingly put you to sleep.

Note: This poem followed the outbreak of COVID-19 pandemic, which has killed a large number of people and altered the conditions of life everywhere.

BUDGET SPEECH

Everything's better than last year
the number of donkeys
                            well   family planning reversed
economic survey shows   the number of donkeys in the country
has increased 5.5 million to 5.6 million
during the fiscal year

opposition appraises the government's claim
       of asinine putsch
       one more augmented reality in place
growth in population
of donkeys
[also buffaloes goats camels sheep]
clapping hooting more clapping
the house drowns in returning waves of bellows
wild screams bleating whimpers and grunts
with a whiff of swearing

agri crops are eaten up   textile
will cover losses shame
opposition accuses the government of donkey rule
donkey rule yes donkey rule
the speaker declares the donkey
unparliamentary
mind you *la langue du parlement* – no donkeys
no donkeys no   in *la langue parlementaire*
           omit donkeys all foreigners from the record

omit and we prorogue *sine die*

somebody pushes a point of order –
prime export to China

ah sell-out for a rash loan to banking flatulence
                         another whispers thirty pieces of silver

omitted his tail shivers   he hasn't a voice only agency
blubbering
(in tones attested for original)
        who stands outside the city gates
        amazed in this tidal desert
by fresh rainwater pits
        and palm leaves

EPISTLE

I

She knocked her foot
against the pile of stones
where she thought was a pavement
and broke her right toenail.
Offered bandaid, she refused.
It would heal, By God, she said.
The city managers laughed.
Stone piles have gone up.
Neighbourhood's gone to the dogs.

I begin to respect my old shoes,
even if they allow for gravel and sand inside;
my socks have pituitary holes.
What's left there to say about footsoles?

Once I found a stone, far over there, walking
lakeside, washed in the round,
with red veins
of the eyes that fell upon it.
It sits here on the bookshelf
by the window,
roiling the view.

Space is cabled, held aloft by pylons.
Early morning's sun is the first corner
I turn. As usual,
the horizon is perpendicular.

II

She just passed through here,
a meteor burning bright
in the emptiness
where breathing time
is a happening, a period.

It's those wars out there
she sent her father and now her son to
which she knows nothing about.

It's those wars in here
her mother and her young daughter
are always hoping and fearing for news.
Every sunrise their questions
and long night lights fizzle out.

The streets were there or not there.
Maybe the trees were there or not there.
This town only built blind alleys.
Their signposts had pointers;
they repeated their names
over and over; led nowhere.

Oh, but what am I to make
of her smile
and wide-eyed staring into the sun?

III

Spare me the next one, love,
I shan't reply in words, lines, dots,
out of inkjet, paper, a white ant virus
gnawing at my word.doc files
that even makes a line straight
as your fine hair frizz,
(real mutt dunking in jello shots);
besides, this place is cold
as the devil's decree for gnomes
that run the everyday machine
cut me off from the gas meter,
regular electricity,
bread I could toast myself;
and don't think they're fighting
WW2 saving anybody anything,
just mocking the act
with their doubles galore;
I have watched the scene for a long time:

'now the barn owl's gone to rest,
why do you sit here alone
by the cold hearth, aren't you tired?'

when I said why, you don't know me –
I'm still awake at this hour
because I'm your conscience
or its unseen shadow
draped in bleeding rags of the new century
and heard this under hot breath:

'you're impossible, eh, we'll kill you;'

so I expect no more answer
either.

MISSING SUBJECTS

> Aliens Issue Statement Asserting That Sex with Them Does Not Spread the Coronavirus. 'In this, as in all matters,' the aliens wrote, 'it's important to follow the science.' By Andy Borowitz.
> – *The New Yorker*, 29 July 2020 (via email)

Whose science? For who would gaily choose
to be crushed between a rock and a
hard place! Alien mode or native,
each state proffers a love formula.
Can we here kiss her (or anyone else) –
even under influence? There's little use
for borders which bruit a fake alternative.
Spaced out they enthuse; couldn't care less
we most want *that* and *that* to overcome
opposites, not so much to be full, or
to consummate body contact with plum
tarts made of white or dark fleshed recipes.
But this hour sequesters fruit from flower.
We can wait. So will the seedbeds, and trees.

A RECKONING

a reckoning and a deal
in the offing –
retracing of steps – and oh
whose fate they seal

the desert worn for ages
ripped with gunshots –
wounding women
chained in cages

once every nut orchard
wished the fruit ripen –
at least the birds were free –
each homestead a postcard

no they cannot flee
those hooded men
parsing body parts with knives –
Pashtu or Farsi

you had a chance to let
them be –
resigned or suffering –
o lord – who will interpret

Note: 'In an interview released Wednesday, [George W.] Bush, from his summer estate in the northeastern US, told German state broadcaster Deutsche Welle, "I'm afraid Afghan women and girls are going to suffer unspeakable harm ... I think about all the interpreters and people that

helped ... they're just going to be left behind to be slaughtered by these very brutal people, and it breaks my heart."'
https://www.voanews.com/south-central-asia/bush-mistake-biden-withdraw-us-troops-afghanistan (14 July 2021 01:15 PM); and also https://www.dw.com/en/george-w-bush-afghanistan-troop-withdrawal-a-mistake/a-58261709 (14 July 2021).

BILLY'S WORLD

So you thought you were at the end
of your tether?
Tented out of town the maimed,
buried your dead,
the final prayers already said

over their bones interred
for good? No use lying.
Billy, my dog, paws into barren
spots every now and then;
searching all of a line without marrow.

And now he unearths some real
dry ones and throws into a wild fire
going here for evening meals.
There's heat & extra as if it were lithium.
He charges ahead with every spark flying.

TESTING GROUND

Roaring down, bodies slashed to pieces,
the avalanche covers up the hundred and thirty-seven
with miles of ice and then it releases

time, unending, for digging, signs of life.
Snow ploughs, depth sensors, hands to heaven
lifted in prayer ask who is at strife

really with whom, while death is the only winner.
Nature's heart melts, though nothing changes
its tough mind. It sheds a blue tear,

makes a lake you must drain too – and divert
the glacial river's course to tame the ranges
in Siachen's domain. There only the most alert

and strong may have a chance, for the peaks
belong to high mountains – wary of intruders –
or to one daring this week's snow blizzard who seeks

whatever lies across one's own warm breath,
the body's agreeable cage, the visible border
of the gunsight. Bless you, soldier: Good Health!

ONWARD

The skies over New York twitter on so,
sandpipers circle up here, settle again ashore.
Herons fly back to the bounteous

pools and eddies of this full river;
water's still-cold edge tells the fish position.
They touch down ever so lightly

poised to snatch a meal,
and dig in with their sharp bills. All happens
in plain surface light that rotates time,

afloat where the ships are offloading sleepy crews,
tins of food, oil & grain, home wares.
Across the first bridge,

local spring figures the short and sweet
sense of things after her dead have been buried.
Cherry blossoms by the roadways are a changing hue:

from white to a light pink to sun-drenched white,
as the air fills with bold voices of school children going by –
with blue words, green petals, songs of tomorrow.

Far away, Thoreau slurps sweet water from the pond
one more time – misses townsfolk talk, is thinking hard:
of course the trees are forthright in April.

SHELTERING IN PLACE

The sky's my only window
smashed by orders to move mornings
don't move don't move evenings
yet on this flat earth dry patch after months of rowing
I feel safer this jungle with or without trees is my home
saltwater fish flow into my hands   the taste in the mouth
rain collects in my shoes
though men in dungarees
women in shorts   weekly raid the silence
of shoreline sands   with questions that feel like
glass broken into the skin   or Atlantic sea sprays
solstice nights long
from rose-petal lips opening   where are you from
even the plain wrong   error ad infinitum
where are you coming from
and I don't know what to say
can't say I've come from nowhere
I'm going nowhere
or haven't anywhere to go
am here only for a bit if you care
but maybe not if my being here
is too jarring   hardly a trope under the sun
for getting together what rag and bone have you
that so irks ballooning philosophies of the now
                all waffle I touch this end falls flat
but places are just
                how time situates you between the remains
before or after   the country lost
that same infernal dread circuits the veins
a sinkhole of terror it sucks out the soul

                          where are those people
                their houses   winter stores
voices of young children fading
none to unfurl red and yellow parasols   only the smell of
charred hair
bodies seared first   then made carbon
so dark every fire in the distance licks life
           through the rubble to the root
so my coming looks like a thing to you perhaps
    and could it be any different   yet now
my going almost nothing

MONTANA

Up in Montana,
they sold me a piece of the moon
last night –

still in my stirrups
   past sundown
      this cold end of the riding trail.

A small amber light from a log cabin
                held the door ajar:
Come in, stranger, she said,
I have horses too, your horse can use some rest.

What can happen again will happen again.
Behind me, moon rocks rise slowly
from the ocean floor,

the land – my own meridian a flickering white

as I pull the reins to notice where I have come:

dumbfounded by those words,
the good tether of a calm between crosswinds

this side of the narrow pass –
                air-wave verbals

of streets in cities west of me,
                            bickering dialects
of packed alleyways east of me.

Who would believe I grew up far, far away?
The occupation armies stole our food and our horses and
our farms, and told us what to think, wear, speak.

        It's not easy to take to pure kindness.
The other side could be just the same dark night.

Wherever it is, old ghosts begin to brown out,
swish their forms off the fir trees.
Look how the wary mustang stays up and sleeps.

INDEX OF TITLES

A Reckoning *152*

Above Balakot *60*

According to the Scriptures *21*

Adam's Peak *116*

All Too Often a Grey Boulder Rolls Down *105*

Amusements for Elinor White *92*

'Any Ideas?' *52*

Arrival *44*

At Eighty-Six *84*

Ban *39*

Beds in the East *71*

Being There *57*

Between the Rivers *66*

Billy's World *154*

Birds in a Tree: An Elegy *55*

Budget Speech *145*

Bulrushes, Normandy *129*

Camp Office *75*

City, West *109*

Composition in Early Summer *76*

Composition in Early Winter *73*

Conversation *122*

Crossing the Alps *104*

Diary *19*

Earthworms *63*
East River *89*
Enlisted *100*
Epistle *147*
Everyday *118*

Facts *114*
Fest *124*
First Information *77*
For Children in Wartime *24*

Garbage News *112*
God Said, Let There Be an End *98*
Grouse *133*

Happenings *95*
How Pale the First Moon of the Year *85*

In Iceland *47*
In Praise of Linseed *37*
It Was Quaking-Grass Awhile *61*

Josephus' Footnote to Historia *90*

L'Objet Trouvé *29*
Laura *50*
Line Rent *34*
Linseed: An Anniversary *38*

Missing Subjects *151*
Montana *159*

N.B. *42*
Ne Plus Ultra *51*
New Orleans, 2005 *62*
No End to Summer *65*
Northern Valleys *80*
Not Moving *88*
Now, Now *74*
Numbers *93*

Occasion *101*
Odesville *131*
Off the Expressway *56*
Onward *156*

Peonies *97*
People *26*
Post *87*

Rescue *82*
River Poem *102*

S Again *130*
Salaam to Ts'ai Lun *33*
Sheltering in Place *157*
Sides *128*
Sister Cities *64*

'Slain Workers Undaunted' *81*
So Welcome, Fuzzy Winter Light *120*
Sonnet After the Tsunami *59*
Spring at the Door *107*
'Stars to Grieve at Pavarotti Funeral' *70*
Still Life *94*
Suggestion *45*
Summer is Here *48*
Sweet Water Only *135*

Taxila / Margalla *22*
Testing Ground *155*
The City Not Being Us *36*
The City without Footpaths *69*
There *46*
They Say, They Never Wrote *111*
To a Query *68*
Tropics *17*
Tryst *91*

Virus Regulation *137*

What Do You Know? *126*
Woodpeckers *72*

Your Dad *127*

Acknowledgements

The poems in this collection were first published in the following journals and anthologies, with minor differences of text here and there:

The Dalhousie Review, The Toronto Review of Contemporary Writing Abroad, Vallum, The Windsor Review, Tower Poetry, The Malahat Review, Journal of South Asian Literature, Maintenant, The Antigonish Review, Envoi, Berkeley Poetry Review, Aries, Obsessed with Pipework, The Brooklyn Rail, Journal of Postcolonial Writing, ARIEL, Kunapipi, Meanjin, Soundings East, Poetry International, Clockhouse, The Maine Review, The Manchester Review, The Wax Paper, Minnetonka Review, Epiphany, North Dakota Review, Grey Sparrow Journal, Solidarity, The Mochila Review, The Nation, Saint Katherine Review, Poet Lore, Index on Censorship, PEN International, Nine Mile Art & Literary Magazine, The South Carolina Review, Poetry London, Naugatuck River Review, Delmarva Review, World Literature Today, Stand, Poetry Salzburg Review, The Milo Review, Gutter, New Statesman, Oxford Poetry, Hampden-Sydney Poetry Review, Fulcrum, Tampa Review, The Louisville Review, Blue Unicorn, SPAN, Acumen, Hamilton Stone Review, Denver Quarterly, Orbis, Slant, Arena, Off the Coast, Blueline, Seam, Kestrel, Dirty Goat, Wasafiri, The Pakistan Times, The Literary Review, The Cape Rock, Up The River, Poetry New Zealand, Water-Stone Review, Poetry Leaves, Southern Humanities Review, The Conium Review, Florida English, New World Writing, Australian Book Review, The Australian, Connecticut River Review, Cordite Poetry Review, Gander Press Review, San Pedro River Review, The Comstock Review, Minnesota Review, California Quarterly, Salamander, Gargoyle, Westerly, Coppertales, Prairie Schooner, REAL: Regarding Arts & Letters, Visions International, Natural Bridge, International Poetry Review, Whisky Jack Press Broadsides (Canada), *Afternoon: Ten to Six* (Rome, Italy & Sudbury, MA: Leconte / Water Row Press, 2001), *Ariels: Departures & Returns* (Oxford University Press,

2001), *Only the Sea Keeps: Poetry of the Tsunami* (Calgary, AB, Canada: Bayeux Arts, 2005), *Battle Runes: Writings on War* (New York: Editions Bibliotekos, 2011), *No, Achilles: War Poetry* (Huntsville, TX: WaterWood Press, 2015), *New Soundings in Postcolonial Writing* (Leiden and New York: Brill/Rodopi, 2016), *Footprints: An Anthology of New Ecopoetry* (Rhydwen, UK: Broken Sleep Books, 2022).

Biography

Alamgir Hashmi has been writing poetry for the last sixty years. He has published eleven books of poetry and numerous volumes of literary criticism. His work has also appeared widely in journals and anthologies and won him high honours, including a long list of citations, nominations, and gold medals. He has been a Rockefeller Fellow and winner of the Roberto Celli Memorial Award. He has given readings of his work at many venues across the United Kingdom, the United States, Canada, Europe, Australia, and Asia.

Hashmi spent his early years in Pakistan, later living in exile for many years in Europe and North America. A former Québécois Kentuckian and a derby fan, he has worked as a professor, writer, editor, and broadcaster, and is generally regarded as a citizen of the world. He has served as a judge of the Commonwealth Writers Prize and as jury for the Neustadt International Prize for Literature. About fifteen years ago, he was made a Life Fellow of the Pakistan Academy of Letters. He is Founding President of The Literature Podium: An Independent Society for Literature and the Arts.